SPACE
FILES

ASTEROIDS AND COMETS

TOP-SECRET DATA

by
Charis Mather

BEARPORT
PUBLISHING

Minneapolis, Minnesota

Credits:

All images are courtesy of Shutterstock.com, unless otherwise specified. With thanks to Getty Images, Thinkstock Photo, and iStockphoto. Front Cover – Paper Street Design, ONYXprj, PremiumArt, Sergey Nivens. Images used on every page – Paper Street Design. 2–3 – Sergey Nivens. 4–5 – Artistdesign29, LuckyStep, sdecoret. 6–7 – Asteroid_Dubois, NASA, ESA, STScI, Public domain, via Wikimedia Commonn, NASA, Public domain, via Wikimedia Commons, Pablo Carlos Budassi, CC BY-SA 4.0 <https://creativecommons.org/licenses/by-sa/4.0>, via Wikimedia Commons, Vadim Sadovski. 8–9 – Andramin, buradaki, Comet_at_perihelion. 10≥–11 – Don Davis for NASA, Public domain, via Wikimedia Commons, Jurik Peter, NASA on The Commons, No restrictions, via Wikimedia Commons, shooarts. 12–13 – Brian Donovan, Godfrey Kneller, Public domain, via Wikimedia Commons, Godfrey Kneller, Public domain, via Wikimedia Commons.tiff, Image on web site of Ulrich Harsh, Public domain, via Wikimedia Commons, NASA Hubble, CC BY 2.0 <https://creativecommons.org/licenses/by/2.0>, via Wikimedia Commons, NASA, ESA, H. Weaver and E. Smith (STScI) and J. Trauger and R. Evans (NASA's Jet Propulsion Laboratory), Public domain, via Wikimedia Commons. 14–15 – CESM I Studio, Leonid Kulik, the expedition to the Tunguska event, Public domain, via Wikimedia Commons, Viacheslav Lopatin. 16–17 – Belish, joshimerbin, sdecoret, Vadim Sadovski. 18–19 - Andrea Danti, Gilmanshin, Giordano Aita, IgorZh. 20–21 – Max Morphine, Vadim Sadovski. 22–23 – NASA – DART – Cámara Draco, Public domain, via Wikimedia Commons, NASA/Johns Hopkins APL, Public domain, via Wikimedia Commons, NASA/Johns Hopkins APL, Public domain, via Wikimedia Commons, Zaleman. 24–25 – 3000ad, Mark Agnor, NASA/Goddard Space Flight Center, Public domain, via Wikimedia Commons, Raymond Cassel. 26–27 – Dinar Omarov, NASA / Tom Trower, Public domain, via Wikimedia Commons, SergeyBitos, Supamotion. 28–29 – Dotted Yeti, Grebenkov, CC BY-SA 3.0 <https://creativecommons.org/licenses/by-sa/3.0>, via Wikimedia Commons, Pavel Gabzdyl, Shoaib_Mughal. 30–31 – Algol, metamorworks, Sergey Nivens. 32 – Sergey Nivens.

Bearport Publishing Company Product Development Team

President: Jen Jenson; Director of Product Development: Spencer Brinker; Managing Editor: Allison Juda; Associate Editor: Naomi Reich; Associate Editor: Tiana Tran; Senior Designer: Colin O'Dea; Associate Designer: Elena Klinkner; Associate Designer: Kayla Eggert; Product Development Specialist: Anita Stasson

Library of Congress Cataloging-in-Publication Data is available at www.loc.gov or upon request from the publisher.

ISBN: 979-8-88509-949-3 (hardcover)
ISBN: 979-8-88822-122-8 (paperback)
ISBN: 979-8-88822-269-0 (ebook)

© 2024 BookLife Publishing
This edition is published by arrangement with BookLife Publishing.

For more information, write to Bearport Publishing, 5357 Penn Avenue South, Minneapolis, MN 55419.

CONTENTS

FOR YOUR EYES ONLY!

The information you are about to read is top secret. Only special agents are allowed **access** to these files on some of the strangest things we know about asteroids and comets. What are the secrets behind these huge, streaking objects?

There are some things in these files that leave even our top scientists scratching their heads. It's up to you to find out as much as you can about asteroids and comets.

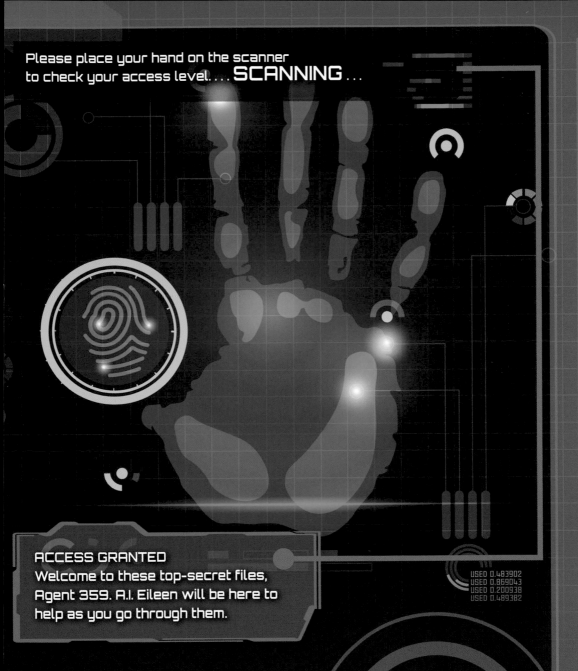

Please place your hand on the scanner
to check your access level.... SCANNING ...

ACCESS GRANTED
Welcome to these top-secret files,
Agent 359. A.I. Eileen will be here to
help as you go through them.

USED 0.483902
USED 0.869043
USED 0.200938
USED 0.489382

A.I. EILEEN:
Hello, Agent 359. You have accessed
our files all about comets and asteroids.
Here, you will find everything you need to
know about these speeding space rocks.

ASTEROID BASICS

A.I. EILEEN:
Asteroids are sometimes called minor planets. Let's begin with some basic information about them.

Asteroids are lumps of rock and metal flying through space. Some asteroids can be hundreds of miles wide. Others may be less than 30 feet (10 m) across.

LUMPY ASTEROIDS

ROUNDER ASTEROIDS

Some asteroids are rounded in shape, but most are more uneven. Their surfaces are usually covered by pits and **craters**.

The asteroid Kleopatra is an unusual shape.

Like a planet, an asteroid travels in an **orbit** around a star, such as our sun. Most asteroids move along a slightly **elliptical** path. It is not quite circular.

A NASA diagram of planet orbits and asteroids

Mars

Earth Sun Mercury

Venus

Jupiter

Most asteroids in our solar system can be found in a place called the asteroid belt. This area between the orbits of Jupiter and Mars contains millions of circling asteroids.

A.I. EILEEN:
Our solar system has more than a million known asteroids.

COMET BASICS

A.I. EILEEN:
Comets are also rocky objects flying through space. But unlike asteroids, comets are made mostly of ice and dust. They travel around the sun in a large elliptical orbit.

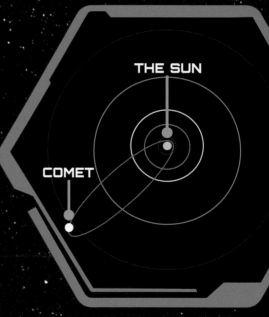

THE SUN

COMET

Most comets are about 6 miles (10 km) across or less. But when a comet gets close to the sun, it changes. The sun's heat turns the ice into gas. When this gas mixes with the comet's dust, it forms a fuzzy cloud that can be hundreds of thousands of miles wide.

GAS TAIL

MAIN ICY AND
ROCKY PART

DUST TAIL

The sun's heat also causes some of the ice to **vaporize**,
creating two tails. One is a white or pink dust tail. The other is
blue and made of gas. The tails are usually between 600,000
and 6 million miles (1 million and 10 million km) long.

THE SUN

As a comet orbits, its tails
always point away from the sun,
each at a different angle. When
comets get close to the sun, their
tails grow and change direction.

DUST TAIL

GAS TAIL

ORBIT OF COMET

9

BELTS, RINGS, AND CLOUDS

A.I. EILEEN:
We know most asteroids are found in the asteroid belt. But what about comets? They come from two different places, both much further from the sun.

ASTEROID BELT

JUPITER

SATURN

URANUS

MARS

NEPTUNE

Short-period comets come from a donut-shaped ring of icy bodies called the Kuiper Belt, just past Neptune. They often take less than 200 years to orbit the sun.

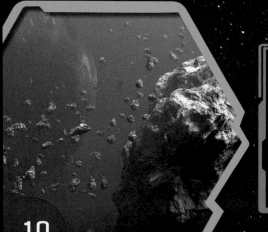

Long-period comets take more than 200 years to orbit the sun. These comets are thought to come from the Oort Cloud—a rounded cloud with trillions of icy bodies at the farthest edge of our solar system.

THE ASTEROID BELT

In 1972, scientists sent a spacecraft into the asteroid belt for the first time. While some worried *Pioneer 10* would be destroyed during its journey, the spacecraft never hit anything large enough to do it damage. There are billions of orbiting rocks in the asteroid belt. However, the objects are so far apart that the chances of a craft hitting an asteroid are very small.

Since *Pioneer 10*, other spacecraft have also passed through the belt safely.

COMET FACT FILES

HALLEY'S COMET

SIZE: about 9 miles (15 km) long, and 5 miles (8 km) across

LAST TIME SEEN FROM EARTH: 1986

NEXT EXPECTED SIGHTING: 2061

LENGTH OF TIME TO ORBIT SUN: 75–76 years

Halley's Comet seen in 1066

EDMOND HALLEY

Halley's Comet has been seen from Earth many times over the last 2,000 years. However, people in the past did not realize the sightings were of the same object. In 1705, Edmond Halley figured out that it was the same comet looping past Earth every 75 to 76 years. The comet was named after him.

Halley's Comet seen in 1986

SHOEMAKER-LEVY 9

SIZE: about 1 mile (1.6 km) wide

LAST SEEN: 1994

NEXT EXPECTED SIGHTING: never

LENGTH OF TIME TO ORBIT JUPITER: 2 years

In 1993, scientists discovered something unusual—a comet orbiting Jupiter instead of the sun. They think that a passing comet was caught in the planet's strong **gravity** about 10 years earlier.

Shoemaker-Levy 9 heading to Jupiter in 21 pieces

Shoemaker-Levy 9 had been broken into more than 20 pieces by Jupiter's gravity. In 1994, scientists watched the pieces, traveling at about 35 miles per second (60 kps), crash into the planet. The explosion shot **debris** about 2,000 miles (3,000 km) into the sky.

The surface of Jupiter after crash

13

THE TUNGUSKA EVENT

A.I. EILEEN:

In 1908, a small asteroid less than 300 ft (90 m) wide rocketed toward Tunguska, in what is Russia today. Though it didn't hit the planet, it made its mark. Let's look at the effect of this near-**impact**.

The asteroid started burning up when it entered Earth's **atmosphere**. People in the area said that they saw a blue fireball flying across the sky. The whole thing exploded with a bright flash about 3 to 6 miles (5 to 10 km) above the ground.

RUSSIA

Forest destroyed ⟶ •

Explosion heard
in this area

ASIA

The explosion set fire to the trees in the area.
However, the fires were quickly put out by the
shock wave from the explosion. This wave was
powerful enough to knock down 80 million
trees in an 800 square mile (2,000 sq km) area!
Some trees that remained standing had their
branches ripped off by the blast. The explosion
could be heard from hundreds of miles away.

ASTEROIDS VS. EARTH

A.I. EILEEN:
How much damage could a Near-Earth Object, also called an NEO, do to Earth? Here's some information about NEOs of different sizes.

SAND-SIZED

Millions of sand-sized bits of rock enter and burn up in Earth's atmosphere every day. These make streaks of light in the sky that we call shooting stars. They don't cause any damage.

When many space rocks burn up in the sky at the same time, it is known as a meteor shower.

HOUSE-SIZED

It would take the impact of a house-sized asteroid to cause major damage. Something of this size traveling at almost 30,000 miles per hour (48,000 kph) would cause an impact big enough to flatten any buildings within about half a mile (1 km).

SKYSCRAPER-SIZED

If an asteroid the size of a 20-story building rocketed toward Earth at 30,000 miles per hour (48,000 kph), everything within 5 miles (8 km) of its impact would be destroyed.

If an object 60 miles (96 km) across or larger struck our planet, its impact would be so powerful that it would make a dust cloud large enough to cover Earth. All life would probably be destroyed.

A.I. EILEEN:
A meteoroid is a space rock that probably came from a broken asteroid or comet. It's called a meteor once it has entered Earth's atmosphere. Most of these burn up in the sky. If the space rock reaches Earth, it is called a meteorite.

17

SURVIVING AN IMPACT

A.I. EILEEN:
A massive meteor impact would be **devastating** for life on Earth. Here is a report from our agents about the biggest dangers and how to survive them.

ON THE SURFACE

The shock wave, heat, and fires caused by a huge meteor impact would destroy everything near it. Anyone who is far enough away to survive would have to worry about what the shock wave might cause next— earthquakes and massive ocean waves called tsunamis. These events could destroy areas the impact didn't reach.

UNDERGROUND

Survivors should immediately seek **shelter** in underground **bunkers**. A meteor impact could cause a dust cloud big enough to cover Earth, blocking all sunlight and making it hard to breathe.

IMPACT WINTER

This dust cloud could last longer than a year. Any plants or animals that survived the impact and the disasters it triggered would soon die off due to lack of sunlight. The lack of light would also send Earth into a very long, cold winter.

A.I. EILEEN:
Thankfully, there are no large asteroids heading for Earth!

THE TORINO SCALE

A.I. EILEEN:
To classify how dangerous different NEOs are, scientists use the levels of the Torino Scale.

LEVEL 0

Objects in Level 0 aren't a danger to Earth at all. These include objects that burn up in Earth's atmosphere and those not near Earth.

LEVEL 1

LEVEL 2

Objects in these levels come closer to Earth than level 0, but they still aren't considered a danger. Scientists track these objects to be sure they continue to pose no threat.

LEVEL 3

LEVEL 4

LEVEL 5

LEVEL 6

LEVEL 7

These levels are for any large objects that may not be an immediate threat but that could have at least a small chance of destroying part or all of the planet in the near future.

LEVEL

LEVEL

The objects in these levels are those that scientists believe will hit Earth and cause extensive damage.

LEVEL 10

A.I. EILEEN:
In 2004, an asteroid rose to level 4 on the Torino Scale—a record high. However, after a closer look, scientists decided there was no danger and moved it back to level 0.

PROTECTING EARTH

A.I. EILEEN:
Although there are currently no dangerous asteroids heading toward Earth, scientists want to be ready. They are working on ways to **deflect** any asteroids that might threaten our planet.

Laser beams focus a lot of energy into a small area, creating intense heat that can split solid objects into pieces. Scientists think they could fire a laser at an asteroid to break it apart or send it flying in a different direction, away from Earth.

DIMORPHOS

DART

Scientists are testing ways to change an asteroid's direction by crashing into it. In 2022, a mission called DART crashed a spacecraft into the asteroid Dimorphos and successfully changed its orbital path. At about 7 million miles (11 million km) from our planet, this asteroid was far enough away to safely run this kind of high-impact test without risks to Earth.

Dimorphos before the DART spacecraft crashed into it

THE DART SPACECRAFT

A.I. EILEEN:
Tests like these are important for learning how to protect Earth from future space threats.

ASTEROID MINING

A.I. EILEEN:
On Earth, we **mine** useful rocks, metals, and minerals. These **resources** are used in electronics, medicines, building materials, and jewelry. But over time, these resources are getting used up and becoming harder to find.

MINING ON EARTH

A.I. EILEEN:
Some people believe that mining asteroids could be a good way to find more of the resources we need.

There are several challenges to asteroid mining. Most of these space rocks have much lower gravity than Earth does. Low gravity makes it difficult for spacecraft to land and stay on asteroids.

Despite low gravity, the spacecraft *OSIRIS-REx* touched down safely on the asteroid Bennu in 2020.

Low gravity also means that asteroids are not held together as tightly. This could result in an asteroid falling apart while being mined. One solution to this problem could be to wrap asteroids in big nets or tarps to catch any pieces that break off.

LIVING ON AN ASTEROID

A.I. EILEEN:
If it is possible to get a spacecraft onto an asteroid, the next question is whether or not humans could live there. Here are some difficulties that humans would need to overcome.

People in space usually spend only a short time in low gravity.

LOW GRAVITY

On Earth, our bodies work against the force of gravity when moving. This effort keeps our muscles and bones strong. If a person lived in the low gravity of an asteroid for a long time, their bones and muscles—including their heart—would not work as hard. The body could become weak and break down more easily.

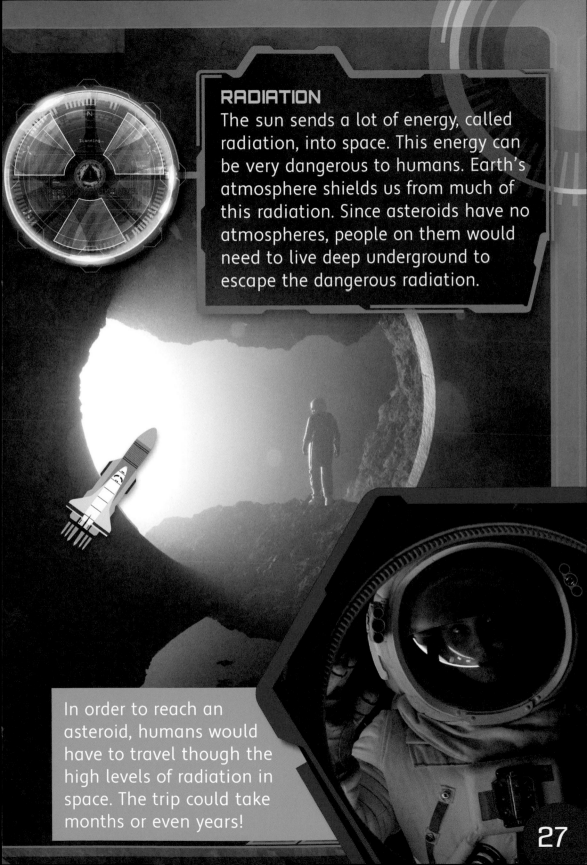

RADIATION

The sun sends a lot of energy, called radiation, into space. This energy can be very dangerous to humans. Earth's atmosphere shields us from much of this radiation. Since asteroids have no atmospheres, people on them would need to live deep underground to escape the dangerous radiation.

In order to reach an asteroid, humans would have to travel though the high levels of radiation in space. The trip could take months or even years!

CATCHING AN NEO

A.I. EILEEN:
Could we catch a passing asteroid
or comet and make it orbit Earth like
a second moon? Let's investigate.

ASTEROID

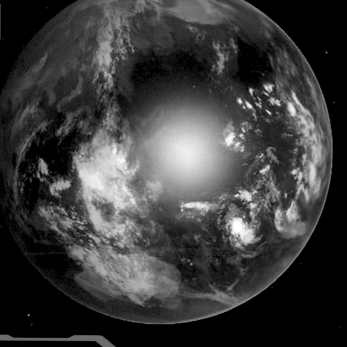

Most asteroids and comets do not come close enough
to Earth to be pulled in by its gravity. Even if one gets
close, most move fast enough to overcome Earth's
pull and would fly straight past. If Earth ever did catch
an NEO in its orbit, it would probably be an asteroid.
Comets move too fast and do not come close enough.

A.I. EILEEN:
While scientists do not think Earth will get an extra moon any time soon, there are other planets that may have asteroids for moons.

MARS MOONS

Mars has two moons—Phobos and Deimos. Both are lumpy and uneven. They seem to be made of rocks that are similar to those found in asteroids.

PLANETARY RINGS

Some planets have rings of rocks around them. These rings may be made of bits of broken asteroids that have been caught in the planets' gravity.

ONE OF SATURN'S RINGS

29

YOUR MISSION

Now that you're up to date on the asteroid and comet files, it's time to find out more. Some secret agents use their new knowledge to come up with ideas to protect Earth. Others figure out ways to make space travel safer and easier. What will you do?

Your most important mission is to pass on your knowledge to others. We're always looking for trusted agents to help us learn more about the strange and interesting side of space. Good luck, Agent 359!

GLOSSARY

access permission to get in somewhere or to see something important

atmosphere the gases surrounding a planet

bunkers strong, well-protected shelters that are usually buried underground

craters pits or holes made from rocks hitting a surface

debris the pieces of something broken or destroyed, such as a space rock

deflect to cause to go in a different direction

devastating causing a lot of damage and loss

elliptical oval-shaped

gravity a strong force that pulls smaller objects toward larger bodies, such as stars and planets

impact a strike or collision

laser a device that creates a very strong and narrow beam of energy

mine to dig underground to find valuable resources

orbit the path something travels around a star or planet; the movement is also called orbiting

resources useful materials

shelter a place that offers cover, protection, and safety

shock waves strong pulses of energy that move outward from an explosion

vaporize to turn a solid or liquid into an airy fog, smoke, or gas

INDEX

READ MORE

Haelle, Tara. *Earth's Place in Space (Science Masters).* Vero Beach, FL: Rourke Educational Media, 2020.

Kingston, Seth. *Comets (Lighting Up the Sky).* New York: PowerKids Press, 2021.

Kruesi, Liz. *Space (Fascinating Facts).* Mankato, MN: The Child's Word, 2020.

LEARN MORE ONLINE

1. Go to **www.factsurfer.com** or scan the QR code below.
2. Enter "**Asteroids Comets Space Files**" into the search box.
3. Click on the cover of this book to see a list of websites.